THE GROSS HUMAN BODY IN ACTION
AUGMENTED REALITY

The MOUTH

A Nauseating AUGMENTED REALITY Experience

Percy Leed

Lerner Publications ◆ Minneapolis

EXPLORE THE HUMAN BODY IN BRAND-NEW WAYS WITH AUGMENTED REALITY!

1. Ask a parent or guardian for permission to download the free Lerner AR app on your digital device by going to the App Store or Google Play. When you launch the app, choose the Gross Human Body series.

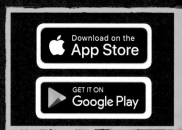

2. As you read, look for this icon throughout the book. It means there is an augmented reality experience on that page!

3. Use the Lerner AR app to scan the picture near the icon.

4. Watch the human body's systems come alive with augmented reality!

CONTENTS

INTRODUCTION
MOUTH CREATURES

Your mouth is filthy. It's a saliva bath for millions of tiny creatures. They share your food, chew holes in your teeth, and make your breath smell like a garbage truck.

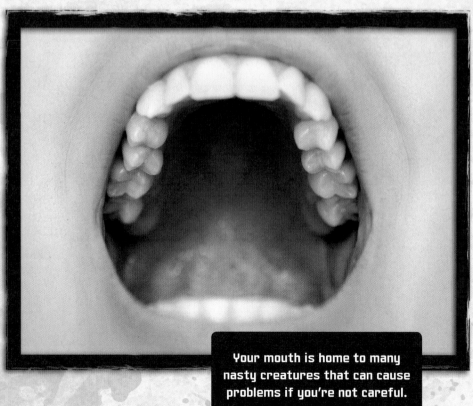

Your mouth is home to many nasty creatures that can cause problems if you're not careful.

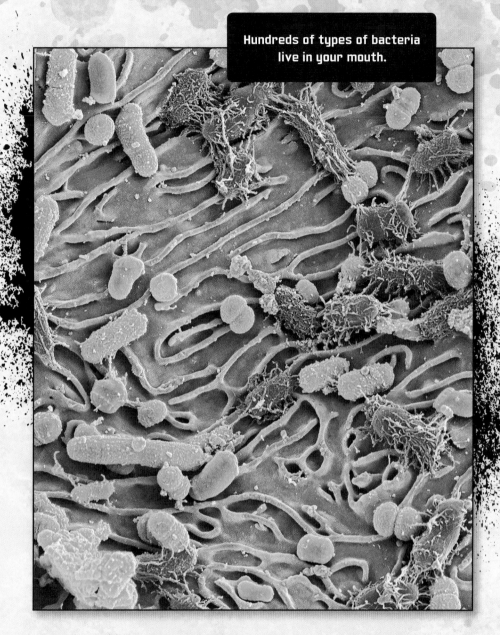

Hundreds of types of bacteria live in your mouth.

Those little creatures can create some disgusting problems in your mouth, such as cavities and sores. From saliva to plaque to bacteria and more, it can be a nasty place. All the more reason to keep that mouth of yours healthy.

SLIMY AND SLOPPY: YOUR SALIVA

You might know saliva by its nickname—spit. It's the slimy stuff that comes out of your mouth when you drool on your pillow at night. It's one of the more disgusting parts of the human body. But spit helps you do a lot of things you wouldn't want to live without—eating, for instance.

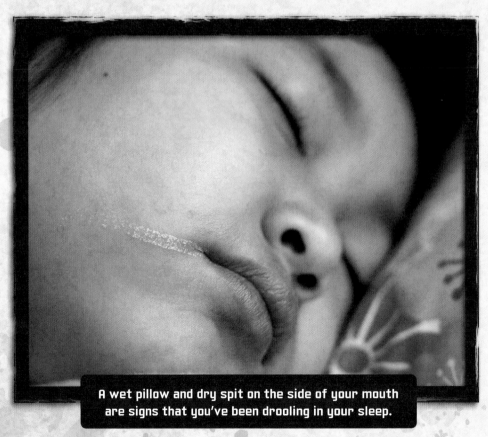

A wet pillow and dry spit on the side of your mouth are signs that you've been drooling in your sleep.

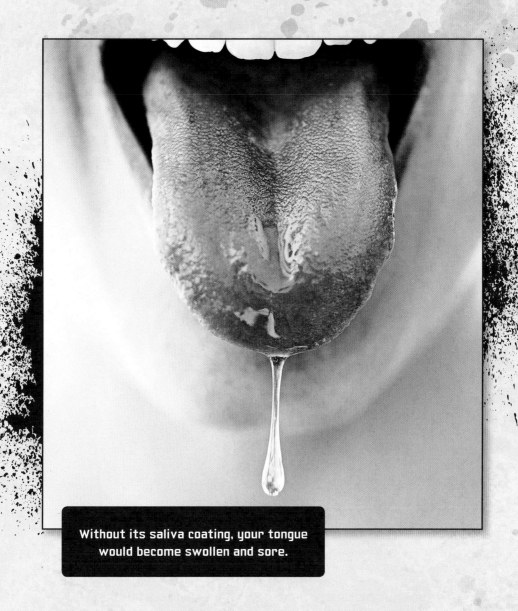

Without its saliva coating, your tongue would become swollen and sore.

The inside of your mouth lives in a bath of spit. You swallow saliva all the time. And thinking about that probably made you swallow just now! Your body makes it twenty-four hours a day, seven days a week.

Spit is mostly water with a few ingredients added in. Mucus makes saliva slimy. The chemical lysozyme kills germs. Another chemical, salivary amylase, breaks down food.

Inside your mouth are hundreds of salivary glands that make saliva. Ever notice your mouth watering right before you take a bite of something yummy? That's your salivary glands in action. You don't even have to take a bite for it to work.

Saliva helps you turn food into lumpy mush that you can swallow.

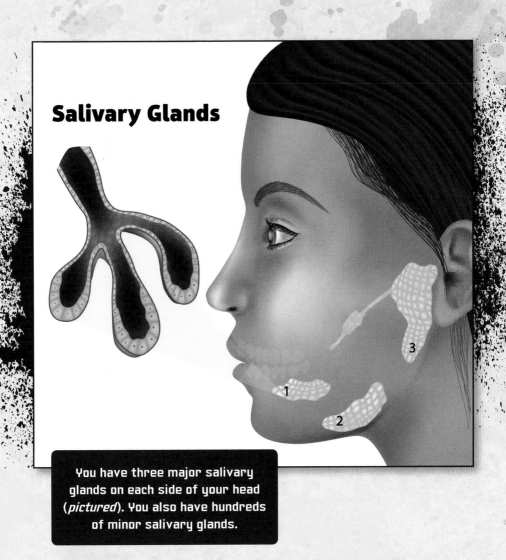

Salivary Glands

You have three major salivary glands on each side of your head (*pictured*). You also have hundreds of minor salivary glands.

Being a walking saliva factory is good. You wouldn't be able to eat without spit. Sure, you could drink. But pizza? Forget about it. Before you can swallow solid food, you need to change it from a dry shape to a mashed-up, gooey ball that will fit down your throat.

When you take a bite of food, your teeth, tongue, and saliva quickly turn it into a wet lump.

This is what saliva does. As soon as you take a bite, it covers every bit of food with a mucus coating. With the help of your teeth and tongue, your bite of pizza becomes a softened-up ball of goop.

Saliva helps your body digest, or break down, food. Salivary amylase breaks down starches—bread and similar foods such as cereal. Think about a blob of half-chewed bread in your mouth. That's salivary amylase at work.

Saliva also helps you taste your food. You have thousands of taste buds on your tongue and inner mouth. When food touches the taste buds, they tell your brain whether the food is sweet, salty, or other flavors. But dry taste buds can't sense taste. Saliva keeps them wet and doing their job.

Saliva is also a key soldier in your body's battle against germs. Lysozyme fights the germs that grow in your mouth. What? You have germs growing in your mouth?! For details, check out chapter 2.

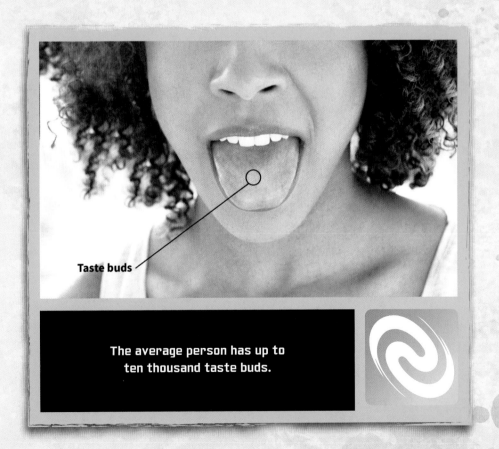

Taste buds

The average person has up to ten thousand taste buds.

WHAT'S THAT SMELL? BAD BREATH

You're huddled close with your friends, telling a joke. Everyone laughs. But suddenly, one of your friends puts her hand over her nose. "Ugh! Someone's breath stinks." What could be more embarrassing than hearing your breath smells like a fuzzy pair of used gym socks? Bacteria cause that nasty odor. Bacteria are tiny creatures that live on your teeth, your tongue, and just about everywhere else.

At times, everyone suffers from bad breath.

This image shows different types of bacteria on a human tongue.

Don't worry about your mouth being a bacteria hotel. Not all bacteria are bad. Some do good things, such as help digest food. But other bugs can cause bad breath and tooth decay. Yikes!

Most bacteria in your mouth are harmless and eat the same food you eat.

Bacteria feast on tiny scraps of food you leave behind when you swallow. Every time you eat a sandwich, you leave behind enough food to feed an army of bacteria. As they chomp away on your leftovers, they produce a stinky chemical called hydrogen sulfur. And when the sulfur escapes your mouth, people will tell you your breath smells like a garbage can.

You can't get rid of all the bacteria in your mouth to avoid bad breath. And you can't stop eating. But what you can do is rely on your body's very own secret weapon against mouth bacteria: mouth amoebas! These little buglike creatures fight bacteria by eating them alive!

An amoeba

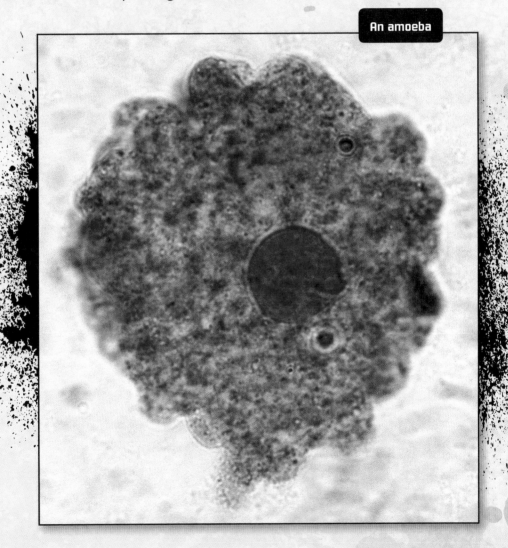

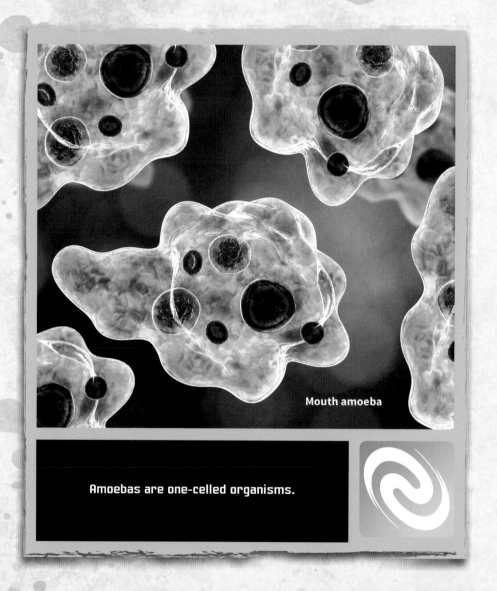

Mouth amoeba

Amoebas are one-celled organisms.

You might be freaked out to hear you have even *more* tiny bugs in your mouth. But mouth amoebas are helpful. Not only do they munch on bacteria, but they also gobble up extra food scraps. That leaves bacteria less food to picnic on.

Mouth amoebas are a cool weapon in the fight against stinky breath. But they can't win the war alone. It's up to you to help by keeping your mouth as clean as possible. A toothbrush and floss are your best weapons. You know about the millions of bacteria living in your mouth, so you know how important cleaning your mouth is. So pull out that toothbrush and get busy!

Keep your mouth clean by brushing twice a day.

CHAPTER 3

ROT AND DECAY: YOUR TEETH

Most people have twenty-eight teeth—fourteen on the top and fourteen on the bottom. Up front are four incisors on the top and four incisors on the bottom. Incisors are sharp for cutting and biting. Next come four canines— one on each side, top and bottom. These pointy teeth help tear chunks of food. Next, you have two premolars and then three molars on each side, top and bottom. These teeth are for grinding up food. Feeling hungry yet?

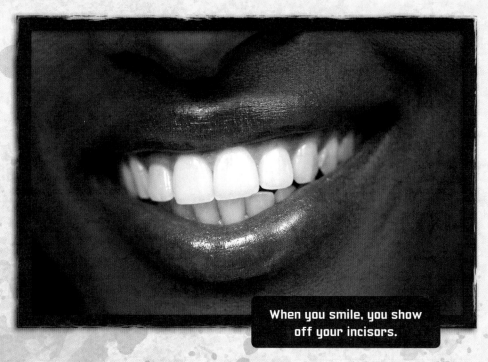

When you smile, you show off your incisors.

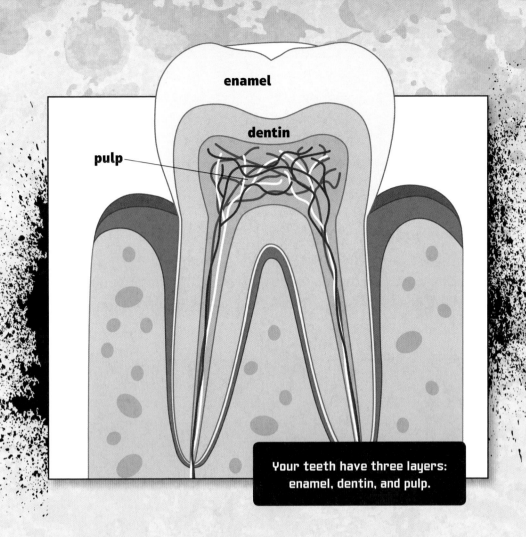

enamel

dentin

pulp

Your teeth have three layers:
enamel, dentin, and pulp.

Your permanent teeth need to last for the rest of your life. Luckily, they're pretty tough. The inside of your tooth is stuffed with dentin, a hard, yellow goop. Dentin gives teeth strength. It's protected by a layer of enamel, the tough outer layer of the tooth. Inside the dentin is the tooth's pulp. It's a soft, sensitive part packed with blood vessels and nerves.

Scrape a fingernail gently along the flat part of one or your teeth. See anything gooey or gross under the fingernail? That's plaque. When plaque stays on your teeth for too long, it hardens. The hardened plaque is called tartar.

Once plaque becomes tartar, you won't be able to get it off by brushing. Or flossing. Only someone at a dentist's office can scrape tartar off your teeth.

Plaque and tartar are pretty harmless if you clean your mouth and see a dentist regularly. The real problems start when you don't do these things. Bacteria in your mouth create acid, a substance that eats away at other things, including your teeth. That's what gives you a cavity, a rotten spot on your tooth.

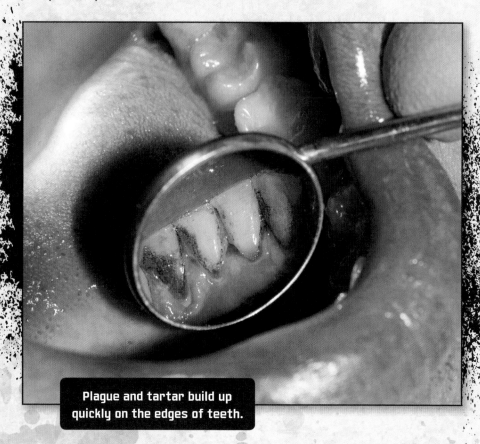

Plaque and tartar build up quickly on the edges of teeth.

When you eat candy, sugar sticks to your teeth. As bacteria break down the sugar, they produce acid that eats into your enamel.

A cavity breaks through the enamel surface of a tooth. When it reaches the dentin, you may feel some pain. If the acid eats all the way to the pulp, you'll definitely feel it.

Cavities are easier to fix the earlier you catch them. Dentists look for brown, soft spots where your teeth are rotting away. To stop cavities from rotting more of your teeth, dentists put in fillings. The dentist scrapes out the rot and any bacteria or food stuck in there. Then the dentist fills in the hole, usually with a soft metal filling.

CHAPTER 4

ERUPTION! CANKER SORES, COLD SORES, AND OTHER PROBLEMS

Ever feel as if a volcano is erupting in your mouth? It's probably a canker sore, not a volcano. Canker sores are small, round sores that grow in your mouth.

It might start with a tingle in your mouth and then become a small, red bump. Before long, it explodes into a full-blown canker sore. The pain is most intense when you eat or drink something spicy, salty, or acidic. When you have a canker sore, you'll want to stay away from these types of foods.

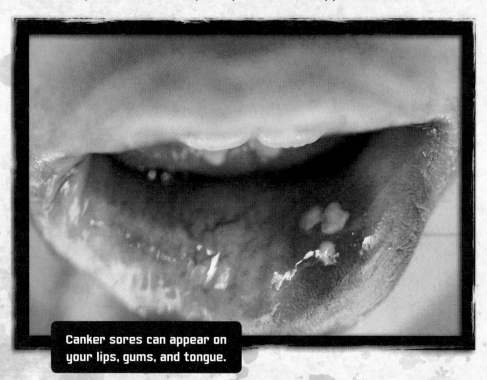

Canker sores can appear on your lips, gums, and tongue.

Canker sores could be caused by allergies, stress, or other problems.

   You should probably avoid getting a canker sore. Unfortunately, scientists aren't even sure what causes them. The immune system is the body's defense against bad bacteria and other invaders. When your mouth gets a small injury, your immune system may attack. The result is—you guessed it!—a painful, pulsing canker sore.

You're more likely to spread a cold sore when fluid begins to drain from the blister. When that happens, don't share your spoon!

But a cold sore is a kissing disease. It isn't caused by a kiss. But kissing—or sharing a glass, straw, spoon . . . well, you get the idea—can spread the virus that causes cold sores. Cold sores are annoying, but they're not dangerous.

Cold sores are nasty little blisters filled with sticky yellow fluid. And it gets worse. Soon the blisters pop, and the yellow goo oozes out and hardens. After about a week, the crusty goo flakes away.

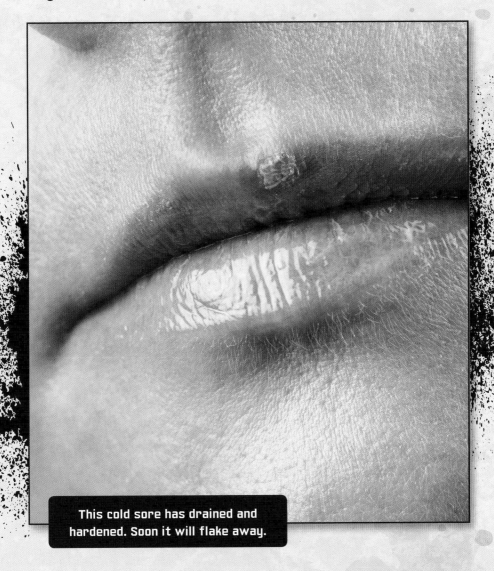

This cold sore has drained and hardened. Soon it will flake away.

You're probably thinking, ew! Could it get any worse than canker sores and cold sores? Funny you should ask. Serious diseases such as chicken pox or measles can settle in the mouth. Luckily, they go away when you get rid of the viruses that cause these diseases.

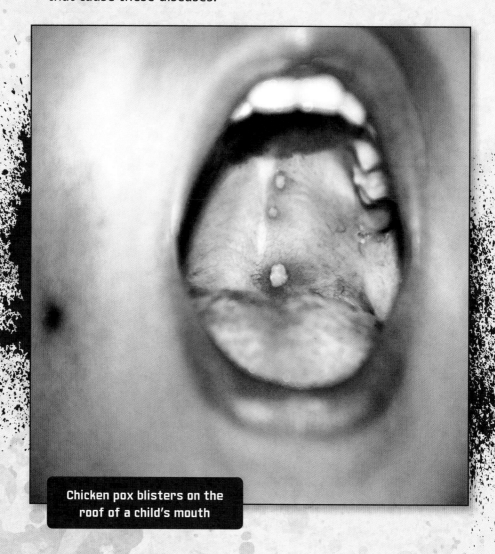

Chicken pox blisters on the roof of a child's mouth

The more you know about your mouth, the more likely you'll be to visit a dentist every six months.

The bottom line is, your mouth is a twenty-four-hour-a-day saliva pool for millions of strange little critters. They even get food delivered every time you eat. It's no surprise that strange things happen inside your mouth. So keep them under control!

GROSS MOUTH FACTS

- The typical mouth makes enough saliva to fill about six cans of soda pop, each day, every day. And guess what? You swallow almost all of it!

- When you sneeze, up to one hundred thousand drops of mucusy saliva come spewing out of your mouth.

- Ugh! You've got halitosis. No, it's not some new and fancy disease. It's just a fancy way of saying bad breath. So grab your toothbrush and get to work!

- Bacteria don't just grow in your mouth. They also grow on things such as toothbrushes if they aren't completely clean. To make sure your toothbrush doesn't become a vacation home for bacteria, replace it every two to three months.

- You might be a plaque and tartar factory. About one in ten kids is! If so, your mouth naturally grows plaque and tartar more quickly than most.

- Some people get canker sores that are 1 inch (2.5 cm) wide. If they're really bad, they might rupture and bleed. Nasty!

GLOSSARY

acid: a sour-tasting substance. Acid made by bacteria in your mouth can eat away at your teeth.

amoeba: a microscopic, one-celled creature that lives inside your mouth and kills bacteria

bacteria: tiny living things that live all around and inside you

immune system: the system that protects the body against disease and infection

mucus: a thick, slippery liquid made by the body

nerve: a thin fiber that sends messages back and forth between your brain and the rest of your body

plaque: a mixture of leftover food, bacteria, and other substances that forms on teeth

saliva: clear liquid in your mouth that helps you swallow and digest food

salivary gland: a small group of cells that makes and releases saliva into the mouth

virus: a microscopic organism that causes disease

FURTHER INFORMATION

Biology for Kids: Bacteria
https://www.ducksters.com/science/bacteria.php

Farndon, John. *Tiny Killers: When Bacteria and Viruses Attack.* Minneapolis: Hungry Tomato, 2017.

Ford, Jeanne Marie. *Dental Hygienists on the Job.* Mankato, MN: Child's World, 2020.

Interesting Facts about Teeth and Dentistry
https://www.childrensdentalvillage.net/patient/resources/interesting-facts/

Leed, Percy. *Guts (A Stomach-Turning Augmented Reality Experience).* Minneapolis: Lerner Publications, 2021.

Mouth Anatomy for Kids
https://www.dentalone-ga.com/mouth-anatomy-for-kids/

The Mouth Facts
http://www.softschools.com/facts/human_body/the_mouth_facts/339/

Settel, Joanne. *Your Amazing Digestion from Mouth through Intestine.* New York: Atheneum, 2019.

INDEX

PHOTO ACKNOWLEDGMENTS

Image credits: Alessandro De Carli/EyeEm/Getty Images, p. 4; STEVE GSCHMEISSNER/SCIENCE PHOTO LIBRARY/Getty Images, pp. 5, 13; Comedstock/ Shutterstock.com, p. 6; David Trood/Getty Images, p. 7; EvgeniiAnd/Shutterstock .com, p. 8; Sakurra/Shutterstock.com, p. 9; frantic00/Getty Images, pp. 10, 22; Science Photo Library/Getty Images, p. 11; BJI/Blue Jean Images/Getty Images, p. 12; Radius Images/Getty Images, p. 14; imagenavi/Getty Images, p. 15; Kateryna Kon/Science Photo Library/Getty Images, p. 16; wilpunt/iStock/Getty Images, p. 17; Rolf Bruderer/Getty Images, p. 18; Bezvershenko/iStock/Getty Images, p. 19; undefined/iStock/Getty Images, p. 20; Busà Photography/Getty Images, p. 21; C.PIPAT/Shutterstock.com, p. 23; Jose Luis Pelaez Inc/Getty Images, p. 24; QUAYSIDE/iStock/Getty Images, p. 25; Moon Safari/iStock/Getty Images, p. 26; yacobchuk/iStock/Getty Images, p. 27. Design elements: EduardHarkonen/Getty Images; atakan/Getty Images; kaylabutler/Getty Images; Eratel/Getty Images; gadost/Getty Images; Freer/Shutterstock.com; Anastasiia_M/Getty Images (green slime frame); Anastasiia_M/Getty Images (green slime blot); amtitus/Getty Images; desifoto/Getty Images; Yevhenii Dubinko/Getty Images; arthobbit/Getty Images; cajoer/Getty Images; enjoynz/Getty Images.

Cover images: Lighthaunter/Getty Images (taste buds); Adam88xx/Getty Images (tongue).

Lerner Publications Company
An imprint of Lerner Publishing Group, Inc.
241 First Avenue North
Minneapolis, MN 55401 USA

For reading levels and more information, look up this title at www.lernerbooks.com.

Main body text set in Aptifer Sans LT Pro.
Typeface provided by Linotype AG.

Designer: Kimberly Morales

Library of Congress Cataloging-in-Publication Data

Names: Leed, Percy, 1968– author.
Title: The mouth : a nauseating augmented reality experience / Percy Leed.
Description: Minneapolis : Lerner Publications, 2020. | Series: The gross human body in action : augmented reality | Includes bibliographical references and index. | Audience: Ages 8–11 | Audience: Grades K–1 | Summary: "From cavities to canker sores to the ingredients in saliva, explore the human mouth in disgusting detail"— Provided by publisher.
Identifiers: LCCN 2019045774 (print) | LCCN 2019045775 (ebook) | ISBN 9781541598096 (library binding) | ISBN 9781728401348 (ebook)
Subjects: LCSH: Mouth—Juvenile literature. | Teeth—Juvenile literature.
Classification: LCC QM306 .H88 2020 (print) | LCC QM306 (ebook) | DDC 612.3/1—dc23

LC record available at https://lccn.loc.gov/2019045774
LC ebook record available at https://lccn.loc.gov/2019045775

Manufactured in the United States of America
1-48000-48678-1/7/2020